The ADVENTURE Toolkit

FRIENDLY ADVICE, FUN AND GAMES FOR GROUPS IN THE GREAT OUTDOORS

GW00402280

The ADVENTURE Toolkit

FRIENDLY ADVICE, FUN AND GAMES FOR GROUPS IN THE GREAT OUTDOORS

DEREK BURDETT

VERTEBRATE PUBLISHING

Copyright © 2008 Vertebrate Graphics Ltd
and Derek Burdett.

Published by **Vertebrate Publishing**.

All rights reserved. No part of this work covered by the copyright hereon may
be reproduced or used in any form or by any means – graphic, electronic, or
mechanised, including photocopying, recording, taping, or information storage
and retrieval systems – without the written permission of the publisher.

ISBN 13: 978-1-906148-04-1

Disclaimer: This book is intended to inspire outdoor leaders with ideas to give
groups an interesting, educational and entertaining time while out in the great
outdoors. It is **not** a training manual for leaders, who must already have the
relevant outdoors leadership qualifications before taking groups out, and it is
not a substitute for a proper training or reference manual for outdoors skills.
The Author and Publishers cannot be held responsible in any way for damage
to property, accident or injury, including death, sustained by any person or
persons following the suggestions laid out in this book.

Photos: Jon Barton, Derek Burdett, David Cannings-Bushnell, Daniel Cardiff,
John Coefield, Chantal Goupil, Alina Hart, Andrew Howe, Oliver Jackson,
Rick Jones, Jerry Moorman, NASA, Andrew Penner, Teresa Pigeon,
Philip Robertson, Amanda Rohde, Rey Rojo, Mark Rose, Marcus Spedding,
Jennifer Trenchard, Sieto Verver, Danny Warren, Ingmar Wesemann,
Graeme Whittle, Jan Will, Lisa Young.

Designed and typeset by **Vertebrate Publishing**, Sheffield,
a division of **Vertebrate Graphics**.
www.**v-publishing**.co.uk.

Contents

Acknowledgements

Many of the ideas, activities and knowledge contained within this book have come from other outdoor professionals, organisations and authors. Where possible I would like to acknowledge those whose work I have used and adapted to put into this book, and those whose feedback has helped this book to develop.

Individuals & Authors

Adam McConkey (First Aid), Colin Mortlock (Safety), David Kolb (Teaching), Elspeth Mason (Reviewing), Fletch (Games), Karl Rohnke (Games), Oscar Tavernini (Rock Identification), Terry Gillespie (Cloud Identification), Roger Greenway (Reviewing).

Organisations & Companies

Health & Safety Executive, Institute for Outdoor Learning, Outward Bound, Plas y Brenin, Rescue Emergency Care, Trangia, World Challenge, Duke of Edinburgh's Award.

I have worked with, and been taught by, many instructors and coaches over the years, and my thanks go out to all of them.

About the Author

Derek Burdett is based in Buxton, in the Peak District, working as an Outdoor Technician for the University of Derby. He teaches activity sessions, lectures to University students and leads overseas expeditions.

Introduction

This book contains some ideas on keeping groups safe, educated
and entertained in the outdoors, from the accumulated knowledge
and experience of 12 years of working in the outdoor industry.

Hopefully this book will be useful as an introduction to leading groups
for those new to the industry, or as an aide-memoire for those with
experience.

I can't really claim credit for much of what's contained in this book.
Thanks go to all those instructors, leaders, teachers and coaches that
I have worked with during my career, and from whom I have 'borrowed'
many an idea for my personal toolkit.

Over the years I have had the opportunity to teach a wide variety of
activities: from bouldering to quad biking, archery to snorkelling,
circus skills to skiing. I believe that variety can be the spice of life,
and it's important to try a little of everything.

Throughout this book I will refer to those leading the activity as leaders,
and those taking part as students.

Derek Burdett

Teaching or Leading?

Teaching or Leading?

Do you describe yourself as a lecturer, teacher, instructor, coach or leader? The specific role will depend on the activity, group and aim of the session. A university lecturer may give a talk about how to surf; an instructor will play games in the surf; while a coach would give feedback after a surfing session. All are equally valid ways to learn about surfing, and a good session may well include all of these aspects.

A good leader will guide the students (while imparting enough knowledge and skill), so that they will safely complete the activity to their own satisfaction, learning in their own way, and having fun doing so.

I once heard someone say that 'A leader is someone who motivates others to achieve a goal'. The motivation is often the hardest aspect, and an attitude of 'challenge by choice' is important. Helping the students set their own goals, while encouraging them to challenge themselves, can give positive results.

When setting goals for the students, they must be **SMART**:

S pecific
M easurable
A chievable
R ealistic and
T ime-bound

...such as getting over halfway up the red route on the climbing wall during the next half hour.

Teaching Methods

IDEAS

Introduction
Demonstration (silent)
Explanation
Activity
Summary

IDEAS covers all the learning styles; the Visual learners from watching the demonstration, the Auditory learners from listening to the explanation, and the Kinaesthetic learners from doing the activity.

Experiential learning is simply letting the students experiment to find out what works, then modifying and building on the skills they have learned for themselves.

KISS

Keep
It
Simple and
Safe

Don't over-complicate the skill, and ensure that students are practising the skills correctly. Practice doesn't make perfect; perfect practice makes perfect.

Using a variety of different ways to teach a new skill allows for different styles of learning, and prevents the students, and leader, from getting bored: questions and answers, lectures, presentations, brainstorming, videotapes, discussions, role-playing, written worksheets, peer feedback, games, and so on.

Lesson Plans

A written lesson plan can help when introducing a skill for the first time, but it must be flexible enough to meet different student needs and learning styles.

Consider

- The **title** of the lesson.
- The amount of **time** required.
- A list of required **materials**.
- A list of **objectives**.
- The **lead-in** to the activity. This is designed to focus students on the skill or concept about to be **taught**. These could include showing pictures or models, asking leading questions, or reviewing previously taught lessons.
- The **instructional component**. This describes the sequence of events that will take place as the activity is delivered.
- **Independent practice**. This component allows students to practice the skill or extend the knowledge on their own.
- The **summary**. This is an opportunity for the leader to review the activity and for the students to pose unanswered questions.
- **Evaluation and analysis**. This allows the leader to reflect on the lesson and answer questions such as; what went well, what needs improving, and how students reacted to the lesson.

Reviewing

Reviewing is necessary to learn. It can highlight what has been done well, and ways to improve. Reviewing can also help to improve team dynamics. The results of a review need to then be applied to be effective.

I hear... I forget

I see... I remember

I do and review... I LEARN!

Kolb's Learning Cycle:

Plan • Do • Review • Apply

Reviews should:
*   have a beginning, middle and end;
*   apply to a range of learning styles;
*   enforce clear rules about behaviour;
*   make it easy to express thoughts and feelings;
*   ensure that learning is recognised and applied.

Planning a Review
*   Why are we doing it?
*   What type of review should be used?
*   When and where should the review take place?
*   How do you run the review?

Ask open questions to encourage a response from the students, and closed questions to try and control the subject. Get information about how they felt and develop plans for the future.

What? • So What? • Now What?

Facts • Feelings • Findings • Futures

Reviewing Styles

- **Marks out of ten** – ask the group to rate an aspect of their performance out of ten.
- **Red and black** – deal out a pack of cards. For black cards, say something that was good. For red, say a way to improve.
- **Traffic lights** – give each student a colour; green (do more of), red (don't do again), and amber (something to start doing).
- **Predictions** – ask the students what they think will happen and compare predictions with actual events later on.
- **On the ball** – ask the students a question. A ball is thrown around the team, and each person who has the ball, answers the question.
- **Hands on** – give the students a statement, for example, 'They listened well', and ask them to place a hand on the student who they think fits the statement.
- **Relativity** – pick an object, such as a rock, and ask the students to position themselves in relation to it considering their contribution. Standing closer to the rock if they were more involved, and standing near to people they worked with.
- **Snapshot** – ask the students to pose and create a 'snapshot' of when they were working well. Ask students what part they are playing in the picture.
- **Video replay** – same as snapshot, but with a video moment that can be rewound and paused.
- **Cards** – have some cards prepared with positive statements written on them. Deal these out to the students and ask them to choose another student who the card fits, and explain why.
- **Round the clock** – have the students pair up and sit or stand in two circles, an inner circle facing out to their partner, and an outer circle facing in. Give the students a question to discuss, choose students to explain the result of their discussion, and then one circle rotates so they have a new partner.

- **Jelly tree** – use a picture of Jelly Babies in a tree, such as the one shown here, and ask the students to choose the one that represents them. Ask if it was different at different points of the activity.

- **Speed reviewing** – similar to round the clock, but in a 'speed dating' style, where they move to a new partner every minute and have to find out their partner's opinions on a selection of topics.
- **Faces** – use a sheet of 'smileys', such as the one shown opposite. Same principle as the Jelly tree: ask the students to choose the one that represents them and ask their reasons why.
- **Karaoke** – the students sing a song to represent how they have performed. This could be a known song (quick review), or they could write their own lyrics (if time allows).
- **Parts of a car** – the students have to choose a part of a car that best represents how they have worked, for example, the **headlights** (leading the way), the **engine** (providing the power).

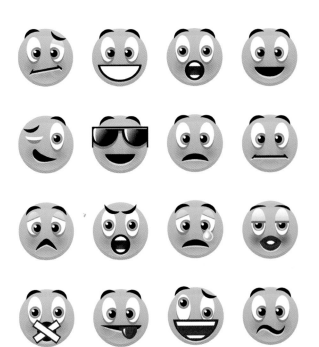

Group Awareness and Safety

Group Awareness
and Safety

A large part of safety comes down to good group management, and the students feeling safe in their comfort zone.

Position of Maximum Usefulness
- Leading from the front to help navigate or when there is a safety issue ahead.
- Leading from the middle so that you can communicate easily with all the students.
- Leading from the side. Putting yourself between a safety concern and the students.
- Leading from the back to watch the team and encourage those at the rear of the group.

Risk Assessment
1. Identify the hazards.
2. Decide who might be harmed and how.
3. Evaluate the risks and decide on precautions.
4. Record your findings and implement them.
5. Review your assessment and update if necessary.

Risk assessments should be undertaken before an activity and continually while the activity takes place, for example:
- **Hazard** – There is a cliff next to the path.
- **Risk** – Students could fall down the cliff.
- **Assessment** – Warn the students about the cliff and safeguard them past it, or take an alternative route.

A leader should always be thinking about safety and reducing risk. A good way to remember some key points is to **CLAP**!

CLAP

Communication
Can the students hear you, or see your signals?

Line of sight
Can you see all of the students, and any potential hazards?

Avoidance
Have you assessed the risks and avoided the hazards?

Positioning
Are you placing yourself in the position of maximum usefulness?

Planning the Day
- Check the weather forecast for appropriate conditions.
- Assess the students' ability, health and fitness.
- Write a route card for any journey.
- Identify skills to be taught and write a lesson plan.
- Inform relevant people of the day's plan.
- Collect the necessary equipment.

Not Losing People
- Counting heads.
- Numbering off, buddy system.
- Meeting places and times.
- Staying in groups of 3 or more.

In Urban Areas

- Easily identifiable meeting points.
- Every group has a watch and knows the time to return.
- Keep valuables and money out of sight.
- Always cross roads safely.

Comfort Zones

These can be explained by using Colin Mortlock's stages of adventure:

Play
Low end of comfort zone

Adventure
In the comfort zone

Frontier Adventure
At the edge of comfort

Misadventure
Outside the comfort zone

During play the students can get bored. They will learn best when having an adventure, and frontier adventure will have the student worried, but satisfied at completing the activity. Misadventure will have the student stressed, frightened and feeling negative about the activity.

Students can feel challenged in several ways: **Physically**, **Mentally**, **Emotionally** and **Socially**.

Each student will feel challenged by different aspects of an activity depending on his or her experience and personality. Activities need to be adapted so that students don't feel in a state of misadventure.

Equipment

Clothing

Sometimes clothing provided by companies to students is of a basic standard. Are you prepared to wear the same clothing as the students? If you do, then you will be aware of how they are experiencing the environment. But if you are cold and wet because the kit is very basic, then you are not able to work to the best of your ability should an emergency occur. If you are not prepared to wear the same clothing as the students, why are you asking them to wear it?

> "There is no such thing as bad weather
> – only bad clothing."
>
> Norwegian Proverb

Safety Equipment

The safety kit carried by a leader is dependent on the activity and some activities will require a more eclectic selection of safety equipment than others, such as sea level traversing or gorge walking. Below are some ideas on useful safety kit.

Extra **clothing** (that will fit the largest member of the team), and hats, gloves, and so on. A spare **water bottle** when the weather is warm, or a **flask** of hot drink when cold. **Emergency food** – muesli bars, chocolate, dried fruit, and so on.

A **group shelter** (KISU) of a size that will fit the whole group. Can also be used as a canoe sail, makeshift stretcher, and so on. **Survival bag** to keep casualties warm.

Knife for cutting ropes in an emergency, and for making sandwiches.
Rescue equipment for rivers or rock – karabiners, slings, prussik loops.
An emergency **rope** for the mountains, to help on steep ground or when
crossing rivers. **Throw line** for activities near or on the water.
Flare/smoke **distress signal** for when at sea.

Spare **torch** and batteries. Appropriate **repair kit** for equipment – bungs,
bolts, cord, duct tape, fabric patches and glue, multi-tool, and so on.
Map and **compass**.

Radios can prove very useful on a variety of activity sessions, such as
the top and bottom of an abseil, or between boats when sailing. Most
people will carry a **mobile phone**, though be prepared for a lack of
signal in the outdoors. **Radio distress beacon** (EPIRB), and **satphone**,
for use at sea and on overseas expeditions.

First aid kit, and appropriate medical supplies when travelling
(anti-malarials, and so on). **Smoke alarm** for use in accommodation
when overseas.

Basic First Aid

I'm no expert on first aid, **and the best thing to do is to take a first aid course**. It can be useful sometimes to teach a few basics and practice scenarios as part of a mountain day, river trip or sailing journey. After all, it could be you who gets injured!

The main aims of first aid are, to **preserve life**, to **protect the casualty** from further harm, to **relieve pain**, and to **promote recovery**.

Other acronyms include:

- **DR ABC**
  Danger, **R**esponse,
  Airway, **B**reathing, **C**irculation

- **MARCH**
  Massive Haemorrhage
  Airway
  Respiration
  Circulation
  Head to Toe

The ABCDE of First Aid

A Assess the situation and person
- Is there a danger to yourself?
- What could have happened to the person?
- What is the casualty's level of responsiveness?

  AVPU
  Alert
  Voice
  Pain
  Unresponsive

B Breathing
- Clear the airway
- Is the casualty breathing?
  CPR
  Initially 30 chest compressions, then 2 breaths and repeat
- Is the casualty's breathing shallow/rapid/rasping?

C Circulation
- Is the casualty bleeding? Apply pressure and raise
- Check circulation (How quickly does blood return to the fingernail after being squeezed?)

D Deformity
- Check body for deformities and other injuries
- Compare both sides of the body

E Emergency Services and Evacuation
- Contact emergency services if necessary
- Evacuate to a safe place if possible

Warm Ups and Manual Handling

Before an activity, students should gently warm up the appropriate muscles for that activity and raise their heart rate ready for action. Warmed up muscles are more flexible, and less susceptible to strains. A 'warm up' gets the brain focused and ready to concentrate on the activity. Also have a 'warm down' at the end to stretch muscles gently and reduce lactic acid build up.

When Lifting:

- use mechanical devices where possible;
- share the load;
- maintain a balanced stance;
- keep the back straight;
- carry objects close to the body.

Expedition Training

Expedition Training

An expedition is defined as 'a journey or voyage for some definite purpose'. This could be describing a three-month trip to a developing country where students will help with community projects, or equally it could be a two-hour paddle down a canal to improve canoeing skills.

Before embarking on an expedition, some level of training is required. The aim is to give the students knowledge and skills, so that they can have a good level of competence and lead parts of the expedition for themselves.

Many aspects of training can be applied to whatever type of expedition the students are completing: Fitness, Leadership, Safety Awareness, and so on. Other aspects of training will depend on the skills needed for the type, and location, of the expedition.

Training can be a combination of demonstrations, such as the use of a Trangia stove, scenarios, for example, one of the team gets lost, and discussions, such as 'How do you keep up morale?'.

A practice expedition often requires the leader to supervise; either accompanying the group, or from a distance. A route card, with planned checkpoints, allows the leader to check the progress of the group.

Training Topics

Training can be divided into four topics: **Safety**, **Equipment**, **Team** and **Individual**. Some examples of subjects that training could cover are shown below:

Safety

- Risk assessments
- Not losing people
- First aid, altitude, malaria
- Condition of transportation
- Accommodation: security and fire risks

Team

- Roles: leader, medics, accountants, and so on
- Working as a team, communication skills
- Cooking, menu planning
- Budgeting the accounts and keeping receipts

Equipment

- Waterproofing personal kit
- Pitching tents and using Trangias
- Rucksack packing and fitting
- Security of equipment

Individual

- Fitness
- Morale
- Water consumption
- Consideration for others and the environment
- Technical skills, such as ice axe use, canoeing

Duke of Edinburgh's Award

The Duke of Edinburgh's Award aims to encourage a spirit of adventure and discovery, by preparing for, and carrying out an adventurous journey, as part of a team.

- Participants must be trained in the skills required to undertake their planned venture.
- Participants must undertake sufficient practice journeys to ensure that they are able to travel and explore safely and independently in their chosen environment.
- The journey may take place on land – on foot, cycle, horse, and so on, or on water – by canoe, sail, rowing, boat, without motorised assistance

The Common Training Syllabus covers:

- First Aid and emergency procedures
- An awareness of risk and health and safety issues
- Navigation and route planning
- Camp craft, equipment and hygiene
- Food and cooking
- Country, highway and water sports codes (as appropriate)
- Observation and recording
- Team building
- Proficiency in the mode of travel

Route and Safety Cards can be downloaded from the 'Useful Stuff' folder at www.theaward.org/involved.

Expedition Cooking

What is a Balanced Diet?

A serving is half a cup, or about thirty grams.

- 6–11 servings of carbohydrate a day such as rice, bread, cereals, noodles, potatoes and pasta.
- 3–5 servings a day of vegetables, especially green, leafy vegetables.
- 2–4 servings of fruit per day.
- 2–3 servings of meat, fish, eggs, nuts, or beans per day.
- 2–3 servings of dairy products including cheese and yoghurt every other day.
- Occasional consumption of fats, oils and sweets.

Menu Ideas

Breakfast: Porridge, cereal, fry-up, scrambled eggs, fruit, pancakes, hot chocolate, tea, coffee.

Lunch: Sandwiches, tortilla wraps, pitta bread, pies, sausage rolls, biscuits, muesli bars, fruit, packet soup.

Main Meal: Curry and rice, stir-fry and noodles, fish cakes (mashed potato, fish and veg coated in flour then fried), stews, chilli con carne, paella, salad and cous cous. Add herbs, spices, salt, pepper, and so on for flavouring.

Desserts: Rice pudding, cake and custard, jam and flat bread (mix flour, water or olive oil and pinch of salt, then fry), hot chocolate and biscuits, fruit.

Cooking on Trangia Stoves

A Trangia stove is a self-contained camping stove that uses Methylated Spirit (Meths) and is typically used by schools, outdoor centres, Scouts and DofE groups. An alternative to Meths is a gel fuel cell from Greenheat, which solves some of the safety issues. Any type of food that can be cooked on a normal gas hob can also be cooked on a Trangia stove.

Fuel Consumption

Trangia's instruction guide recommends 0.5 litres of meths for cooking per person per week. Weather conditions and the type of food chosen, for example, boiled potatoes vs. instant mashed potatoes, affect fuel consumption. Cooking times can also vary depending on altitude. It is always advisable to take spare fuel.

Saving Fuel

Using the pan lid saves fuel. The heat can be adjusted with the simmer ring on the burner, which also saves fuel. Use fuel remaining in the burner for making coffee, tea, or heating water for washing up.

Safety

Meths can burn with a clear flame, so care should always be taken with any naked flames. Keep the fuel a safe distance from lit stoves and carry the brass burner to the fuel to refill it, preventing the risk of pouring fuel into a lit stove. To prevent spillage of fuel, never completely fill the burner: ¾ full is sufficient.

Access Land

You are welcome to walk over this open country, which has
been designated as access land under the
Countryside and Rights of Way Act 2000

Motor vehicles, cyclists or horse riders must
keep to their legal rights of way

To fully enjoy your visit and help protect the countryside for
everyone, please follow the Countryside Code:

Be safe - plan ahead and follow any signs
Visitors are responsible for taking proper care of themselves and any
accompanying children or dogs.

Consider other people
Please take care not to disturb other people, livestock or wildlife. Leave
gates and property as you find them.

**Protect plants and animals and take your
litter home**

Keep your dog under close control
Keeping it on a short fixed lead will prevent disturbance to livestock and
wildlife – this is a legal requirement when near farm animals and from 1st
March to 31st July.

Local Restrictions may apply: For details please ring the
Open Access Helpline 0845 100 3298
website www.countrysideaccess.gov.uk

Guard against fire
Stub your cigarette out carefully, not on the peat or vegetation.

Peak District National Park Authority
Tel 01629 816200
www.peakdistrict.org

PEAK
DISTRICT

Get a grip!

Walkers only.
Thank you

PEAK!

Environment

Access

 Access land in England and Wales is marked on Ordnance Survey maps, and is shaded yellow. Stiles and gates that are access points are marked with the symbol shown here.

What you **may** do on access land: Most recreational activities that are carried out on foot, such as walking, bird-watching, climbing and running.

What you **may not** do on access land: Water sports, camping, cycling, horse riding, motor sports and the driving of any vehicle other than a mobility scooter or buggy.

Countryside Code for England and Wales (new in 2004)
- Be safe, plan ahead and follow any signs
- Leave gates and property as you find them
- Protect plants and animals and take your litter home
- Keep dogs under close control
- Consider other people

Scottish Outdoor Access Code (new in 2004)
- Respect the interests of other people
- Care for the environment
- Take responsibility for your own actions

Cloud Identification

1

Is the cloud a layer or a heap type?

Layer or sheet of cloud
Featureless base, edges often indistinct, no puffiness.

Clean white, high level (same levels as jet contrails), partly transparent, no precipitation reaches ground.

Sky partly covered with delicate streaks or fibrous patches, "mares' tails" or "Christmas angel hair".

Continuous thin veil, usually produces "ring" around the sun or moon.

Cirrus (Ci)   **Cirrostratus (Cs)**

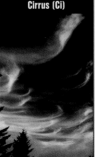

**Heaps, rolls, puffs,
or waves of cloud**
Edges of rolls and puffs
often sharply defined.

See overleaf...

Dirty white or grey, middle
troposphere (below
contrails but above light
aircraft), sun visible only as
hazy patch ("ground glass
sun"), usually no
precipitation.

Altostratus (As)

Uniform dull grey layer with base at low level
(same levels as light aircraft).

Overcast, thick, dark grey,
usually covering whole sky,
completely hiding sun,
continuous or intermittent
rain or snow.

Nimbostratus (Ns)

Very low, light grey,
often thin and "burns off"
during the day, only light
drizzle or no precipitation.

Stratus (St)

Cloud Identification

2

Is the cloud a layer or a heap type?

Layer or sheet of cloud
Featureless base, edges often indistinct, no puffiness.

Dirty white or grey, middle troposphere (below contrails but above light aircraft), patches of distinct rolls or puffs or waves.

Altocumulus (Ac)

Clean white, high level (same levels as aircraft contrails), patches of small distinct puffs or ripples.

Cirrocumulus (Cc)

Large low rolls with puffy edges but very little vertical extent. Sometimes organised into "streets" with clear avenues between, no precipitation in summer but light snow flurries in winter.

Stratocumulus (Sc)

Heaps, rolls, puffs, or waves of cloud
Edges of rolls and puffs often sharply defined.

Flat grey, bases at lower levels (same levels as light aircraft).

Puffy "cauliflower" clouds of fair weather, no precipitation, usually covering less than half the sky and having only a little vertical extent, bright white tops with sharp edges.

Cumulus (Cu)

Rapidly growing heap clouds with considerable vertical extent and sharply rounded white tops, likely to produce vigorous brief showers or snow flurries.

Cumulus congestus (Cu+)

Very large convective cloud with great vertical extent, rising to aircraft contrail levels with fibrous anvil top. Produces heavy showers, thunder, lightning and hail.

Cumulonimbus (Cb)

Activities

Tree Hugging

This task needs to take place in an area of woodland or forest. Pair up the students and blindfold one of the pair. The sighted student carefully guides their partner to one of the trees. The blindfolded student has 20 seconds to touch the tree, then is lead back to the start point. The student has to find the tree that they were hugging. Repeat the game for the second student.

Natural Art

Each team is given an equally sized, marked out area of ground. The task is to produce a piece of art within this 'picture frame' only using natural materials lying on the ground. Alternatively, create a map of the hills, coastline, section of rapids, cave system, and so on.

Eyes Shut

In an appropriate part of the countryside, ask the students to sit down, shut their eyes and describe the sounds and sights they have at home. Then open their eyes and describe what they can see and hear.

The Leaning Tower of Rocks

Where rocks are lying on the ground, such as at a beach, on the inside of a river bend, or at the bottom of a crag, the students must try to build a tower of rocks. The tower will consist of single stones stacked on top of each other to form the highest tower.

Rock Identification

Follow the questions to identify the rock type.
Vinegar is needed to identify some rocks.

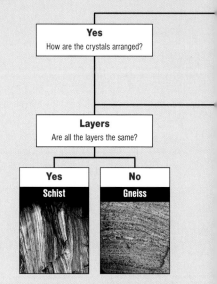

Yes

How are the crystals arranged?

Layers

Are all the layers the same?

Yes	**No**
Schist	Gneiss

Do you see many crystals in the rock?

No
Do you see sand grains or pebbles?

See overleaf...

Scattered
What colour are the crystals?

Light
Does it fizz with vinegar?

Dark

Gabbro

Yes

Marble

No

Granite

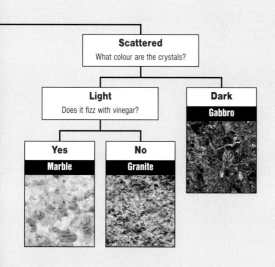

Rock Identification

2

Follow the questions to identify the rock type. Vinegar is needed to identify some rocks.

Previous page...

Yes
How are the crystals arranged?

Yes
What size are the particles?

Holes
What colour are the holes?

Small Grains	**Coarse Grains**	**Large Pebbles**
Sandstone	Gritstone	Conglomerate

Light	**Dark**
Tufa	Scoria or Pumice

Thanks to **Oscar Tavernini**

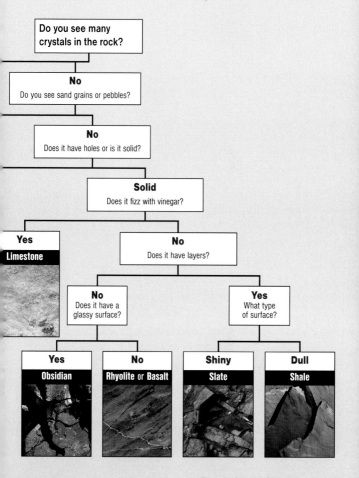

Do you see many crystals in the rock?

No
Do you see sand grains or pebbles?

No
Does it have holes or is it solid?

Solid
Does it fizz with vinegar?

Yes
Limestone

No
Does it have layers?

No
Does it have a glassy surface?

Yes
What type of surface?

Yes
Obsidian

No
Rhyolite or Basalt

Shiny
Slate

Dull
Shale

Games

Games

Playing games is fun, and when you're having fun, it's easier to learn. Games can also reinforce whatever aspect of the activity is being taught at the time; for example, playing a ball game in kayaks after learning the sideways draw stroke (picking up the ball without reaching out and capsizing), or a race on mountain bikes where the slowest person wins, after talking about balance and control.

With all games, the rules are there to be changed to suit the environment and the students. Making up new rules while playing the games is part of the fun. Rules about safety and boundaries to the playing areas must be clearly explained.

Consideration must be given to the following:

- Hazards in the area, such as cliffs, roads, rivers, weirs and trees.
- The size of area being used. Ensure that the area can be marked appropriately so that everyone knows the boundaries and precautions taken so that students can be recalled if necessary.
- Ensuring that the students know how to get help if required. Over very large areas, it may be appropriate to use a 'buddy system' where students are paired up and responsible for each other at all times.
- Time limits and 'End of Game' signals. If a whistle can mean more than one thing, make sure that the whistle blasts are clear enough to be heard and understood.

- Ensure that the students are involved most of the time. If they are 'out' or 'caught', it should not be long before they are be reinstated, join another team or are in some way involved again.

Many games can be adapted so that they can be used in a variety of activities:

- football/netball/basketball;
- tag or 'it'; for example, sailing (using a rubber duck thrown into the boat);
- follow-the-leader outdoor activities, such as skiing, kayaking;
- stuck in the mud, dropping the windsurf sail, until 'tagged' and set free, for example;
- races, such as the fastest bouldering traverse or the quickest reverse canoe paddling.

Challenges can be added to make an activity move interesting, or to compete against other teams:

- having points systems for elements of an activity; for example, 10 points for standing up in a kayak;
- making a map and comparing it with a master map, or creating a map that other students must use, for example caving, orienteering, sailing;
- remembering knots or other information that can be tested later.

Travelling Games

Games such as I Spy, A–Z, song lyrics, jokes and logic puzzles can help pass the time while walking or travelling.

Guess Who

Students pick a subject, such as actors, athletes, 'The Simpsons' characters, and think of a person. Other students take turns to ask questions with a Yes or No answer. If they get a Yes, then they ask another question, a No and the next student can ask a question. The person who guesses correctly starts the game again.

More Games

Icebreakers (see overleaf)
Games to get students interacting and learning more about each other.

Energisers (see page 53)
To wake the students up at the start of an activity, keep them warm, or just for fun.

Trust Exercises (see page 66)
To get the students working well before climbing or other activities, where trust is needed.

Evening Activities
For evening activities, there are team games (see page 55), quizzes (see page 82), Mini Olympics (see page 91), hunts (see page 95) and performances (see page 98).

Icebreakers

Ordering

The team are asked to stand in a straight line. They are given criteria to sort within their team - such as shoe size, height, colour of clothing or alphabetically by name. They then have to put themselves in order in their line. The ordering process can be repeated with restrictions such as silence, or only the student with the hat is allowed to speak. The criteria for the order can include information about the student, such as number order of brothers and sisters, A–Z order of street they live on, and so on.

Human Knot

An even number is needed. If there is an odd number, one student can be nominated as the 'leader'. The students stand in a circle, facing in, with their shoulders touching. Each student raises their right hand and takes hold of another person's right hand, but not someone next to them. Then the team raise their left hands and take hold of a different person's left hand, this time it can be someone next to them. The aim is to now untangle, without letting go, until a circle is formed.

The students are allowed to adjust their grip, so that injuries are avoided, and must take care when climbing over, or under other people. It may be that a figure of 8 is formed, or two separate circles.

Similarities

A question is asked to the team with a discussion to follow: for example, are you more like summer or winter; a 4×4 or a sports car; a cat or a dog; a hole punch or a stapler?

The students then move to join those with the same choice.

Speed Ring/Team Juggle

The team stands in a circle and a ball is thrown from one team member to another without repeating anyone in the team. On receiving the ball the sequence of names of people the ball has been thrown from is to be repeated aloud adding the receiver's name on to the list. The ball is not to be passed to a member of the team who has already received it.

Group Sit

The team stand in a circle with their shoulders touching, then turn 90° to their right, and take two paces toward the centre of the circle. The students must then bend their knees and sit on the lap of the person behind them. Several attempts may be needed. The next stage is to remain sitting, and to all raise their right foot and move it, then their left, and so on.

Similarity Charades

Divide into smaller teams. Each team discusses their similarities and acts them out for the other teams to guess.

Tiny Teach

The students pair up. Ask them to teach each other something new that will only take a few minutes to learn. The lesson could be a skill, like how to use a blade of grass as a whistle, or it could be intellectual knowledge, like a motto in Latin. After they have all been taught, ask the pairs to demonstrate what it is they have learned.

I've Never Ever?

The students sit in a circle, with one student standing in the centre. That student makes a statement starting with "I've never ever ..."; for example, "I've never ever been canoeing". Everyone who has done whatever the statement relates to must swap places. The slowest student is left in the middle and will have to make a new statement. If the statement made by

Penguin Race

Everyone stands in a circle. The leader
starts to tell a story about penguins, and
how we're going to have a race like the
penguins do, with the actions.
Demonstrate and practice the actions,
then have a 'race' – in other words, the
students do the actions when called out.

- **Everyone must stand like a penguin:**
  Heels together, toes out, arms straight down.
- **Walk like a penguin:** Shuffle on the spot
  from foot to foot, while slapping thighs to
  make the sound of flippers against the snow.
- **Run like a penguin:** Shuffle and slap faster.
- **Take a left bend:** Raise right leg slightly
  and hop on the spot around to the left.
- **Take a right bend:** The same but other leg and direction.
- **Water jump:** Hold nose, jump up in the air, make 'bubble bubble'
  noises while bending knees and sinking down.
- **Ski jump:** Push with pretend ski poles, crouch down and make
  'shush' sound as if sliding down slope, jump up and hold position as
  if flying, make 'thump' sound as if landing.
- **Snowboard course:** Stand sideways as if on a snowboard, hop
  180°, then back 180°, then make a big jump in the air while bending
  the knees, pretending to grab the board and saying "Yo Dude".
- **Passing the posh crowd:** Stand up straight, politely clap hands and
  say "Oh yah, terribly spiffing".
- **Passing the rowdy crowd:** Shake fist and shout "C'mon".
- **Worm on the course:** Screech to a halt, hockey player style, hold
  out arm and make wiggly worm motion with index finger while saying
  "eek eek".

the student is false, and they had done whatever it was, then they are given a forfeit, such as singing a song, and the same applies to those who should have moved and didn't.

Circle the Circle

The group stand in a circle, holding hands. Two members join hands through a loop of rope. The loop must travel around the group, with team members climbing through the loop, but without breaking the circle. Two loops sent in different directions, or smaller loops, can make it more interesting.

Energisers

Duck, Duck, Goose

The team sit on the floor in a circle. One student walks around the outside of the circle, gently touching each person on the head and saying 'duck' as they do. When they touch someone and say 'goose', that person must get up and chase the caller. If the chaser tags the caller, then the caller starts again. If the caller gets around the circle and sits in the chaser's space without being tagged, the chaser becomes the next caller.

Watch out for students being too aggressive when they are touching the heads, and it may be necessary to intervene if a particularly slow person becomes the caller.

Fletch Ball (invented by Fletch?)

The students are divided into two teams. A point is scored when a ball has been passed around the team and each team member has held the ball. While holding the ball, the student cannot move, and cannot be tackled, as it is a non-contact game. The opposing team tries to get the ball so that they can start to pass it around their team. Once a team loses possession, they must start from the beginning again.

Simon Says

This classic game can get as silly and as energetic as the leader wants. The leader says an action, such as "Hop on one leg", but the students only do the action if the leader starts the command with "Simon says". Those who start the action when Simon **didn't** say it are out of the game. It's best to start the game with lots of easy commands so that everyone is warmed up before students start getting knocked out of the game

Evolution

All students start off as amoeba, and move around (saying "wibble") to find another amoeba. Once they have, they play 'paper, scissors, stone'. The winner moves up the evolutionary ladder to become a frog ("Bonjour"). When two frogs play, the loser goes down one level to amoeba, the winner goes up to rabbit ("What's up Doc?"). Rabbits go up to Homer Simpson ("D'oh!"), and Homer changes into James Brown ("I feel good..."). When two James Browns play, one stays, while the other moves down a level.

Star Game

Each team stands in single file facing toward the centre of a circle, like the spokes on a wheel. The team is then numbered off with one being at the start of the line. When the leader shouts out a number, the corresponding student must turn left and run around the outside of all the teams until at the back of their team. Then they have to crawl between the legs of their team-mates, until they can touch an object placed at the centre of the 'star'. Points are awarded for first, second and third place. Having more than one number called makes for interesting races. Probably not suited for surfaces that could cause damage to the students' knees or elbows, such as rough tarmac.

Port and Starboard

The playing area represents the deck of a boat. The end where the Leader stands is the bow (front of the boat), right side is starboard, left is port, back is the stern. When the leader calls out a command, or direction, the last student to move to the correct area, or do the command, is out.

Other commands can include:

- **Mind the boom:** Everyone lies on the floor.
- **Captain on deck:** Everyone stands to attention, salutes the leader and says "Aye Aye Cap'n".
- **Man the oars:** Everyone moves to the sides and starts rowing.
- **Crow's nest:** Students pair up, and one lifts the other on their back.
- **Hoist the sails:** Everyone moves to the centre of the boat and starts pulling the sails up; and so on.

Team Games

Kick Cricket

1. Two teams (one team of fielders, the other kickers).
2. A Leader bowls the ball underarm.
3. The kicker kicks the ball.
4. The kicker then runs to the far stump and back to their wicket.
5. The fielders throw the ball and try to hit the runner on the legs, before they get back to the wicket to put them out.
6. A fielder cannot run with the ball, but can throw it at the runner or to another fielder.
7. If a fielder catches the ball before it bounces the kicker is out.
8. When all the kickers are out, all change.

Sponge Volleyball

Each team has sponges in a bucket of water and the players hold small plastic containers on their heads. One team serves by throwing a sponge over the net, if the sponge lands inside the court they score a point, if the sponge is caught in a container (without moving the container from their head) the other team serve.

Many other games can be played using wet sponges instead of balls, such as **Dodge Sponge**. In this game, two teams each have a playing area and throw sponges at each other. If hit, they're out, but if they catch a sponge, another player comes back in. First team all out lose.

Tower Ball

End Zone
Main Area
Main Area
End Zone

Requires four marked out areas as shown in the diagram. Each team stands in one of the main playing areas, with a catcher in the opposite end area. The sizes are flexible, but the distance has to be such that the least proficient student is able to throw the ball to the catchers. The ball must be passed among at least 3 people before at attempt is made at throwing it to a catcher. If successful, the thrower joins the catcher in the end zone. The game ends when either the time is up, or the whole team has got to the end zone.

Ultimate Frisbee

Set up two markers for the ends of each goal line. Each team starts on their goal line. The players can move once one player starts the game by throwing the Frisbee toward the opposition's goal line. The other team either catch the Frisbee or pick it up and the game continues. Once a player is holding the Frisbee, they cannot move from that position, and can't hold the Frisbee for longer than 10 seconds. It's a non-contact game and players cannot steal the Frisbee out of another player's hand. If the

Frisbee lands on the floor or goes out of bounds, the team last to touch it loses possession to the other team. When the Frisbee passes over the goal line and is caught, a goal is scored and the winning team start the next game off.

Crab Football
Football rules, but all players are in the crab position: back towards the floor, supported on hands and feet, with feet facing forward.

Dwarves, Wizards, Giants
This is a team version of the game 'Paper-Scissors-Stone'. To win, Dwarves tickle Wizards, Wizards frazzle Giants, and Giants squash Dwarves.

Dwarf
Squat down to make yourself shorter. Wave fingers as if tickling, and say "Tickle, tickle, tickle".

Giant
Stamp feet, arms raised in frightening posture making growling/roaring sounds.

Wizard
Stand normally but with arms outstretched as if casting a spell. Make appropriate spell casting noises, such as "Kazam!"

Each team has a home line. They decide on their character and approach the other team so that each team faces off in the middle. On the count of three, both teams act out their character. The winning team chase the others and tag them before they reach their 'home'. Tagged people join the other team. Keep going until one team is eliminated.

Wide Games

A **wide game** is an outdoor activity, usually in a wide area of woodland or other countryside, often between two or more teams who have to achieve specific objectives in order to win the game.

Consideration must be given to:

- The hazards in the area, such as cliffs, roads, rivers, and so on.
- The size of area being used. Ensure that the area can be marked appropriately so that everyone knows the boundaries and precautions can be taken so that students can be recalled if necessary.
- Ensuring that the students know how to get help if required. Over very large areas, it may be appropriate to use a 'buddy system' where students are paired up and responsible for each other at any time.
- Time limits and 'End of Game' signals. If a whistle can mean more than one thing, make sure that the whistle blasts are clear enough to be heard and understood.
- Ensuring that the students are involved most of the time. If they are 'caught', it should not be long before they are be reinstated, join another team or are in some way involved again.

Spotlight

The team are given a start point, and the aim of getting to the leader without being caught. While the leader counts down from five to one, the students can move. After one, the leader shines their torch, and any students who can be seen moving are 'out'. Once the torch is off and the countdown begins again, the students can once more move.

Camouflage

The students are taken to a start point, at which the leader will stand. The students are then given the opportunity to hide while the leader shuts their eyes and counts down from ten to one.

Any students who are not camouflaged enough and spotted are then 'out' and join the leader. The leader then shouts 'camouflage' and briefly holds up their hands with a number of fingers showing.

The students are then called back in, and those who can correctly say how many fingers were raised gain a point, then the game is repeated.

Foxes and Hounds

One team are the chasing team (the hounds) while the others are the hiding team (the foxes). The foxes are given a few minutes head start. Touch rugby rules should be applied: being touched by a hound means that the fox must return with the hound to the leader, and a proper rugby tackle is not allowed. After a pre-arranged time, all students must return, and the roles are reversed. The team with the fewest students caught are the winners. Again there are many variations on this theme.

Capture the Flag

The students are divided into two teams. At each end of the playing area is a flag, and in the centre is the jail. Once the game begins, the teams are free to try and get the other's flag. If a student is caught on the other team's side (ensure that tagging doesn't turn into rugby tackling!) this player must sit in jail until a time penalty has passed. To win the game you must capture the other team's flag and return it to your own side without being captured. It is up to the team on how they want to place their members. It's usual to have two players guard the flag and one player as the jail guard. Two or more players stick around and help provide the defence, the rest go for the flag.

This game can be played with two small pots and a lit candle in each pot instead of a flag. Each team tries to put out the other team's candle by sneaking up and blowing it out before being caught.

Kim's Game

Before the game, pick up a few objects (10+) which the students may find lying about in the area, such as nuts, holly leaves, berries, sweet wrappers, stones and lay them out. The teams or individuals must find objects that are close matches to the objects you have collected. You can either display or hide your collection so that the players can or cannot come back and refresh their memories. The team with the display best matching the original wins.

Tasks

Blind Square
The students are given planning time to work out how they will form a square with a large loop of rope while blindfolded. Then the team is blindfolded and the rope is placed into their hands. Ensure that students don't walk into obstacles while they are blindfolded.

Turn the Carpet
The students stand on a piece of tarpaulin. Together they have to turn it over without stepping off it.

Shrinking Life Raft
The students all try to stand on a piece of tarpaulin. Each time they succeed, the material is folded to a smaller size, and they try again.

Team Skipping
Given a long piece of rope, the team tries to jump the rope simultaneously – starting with one or two people and gradually working up to the whole team.

Long Distance Clove Hitch
The team members have a clove hitch displayed to them. They all get to practice this on short pieces of rope. They are then told to tie a clove hitch around a tree or pole but are unable to come within 2 metres of the tree/pole, indicated by markings on the floor.

Magic Cane

The students form two lines facing each other. Each student holds their hands out at waist height with the index fingers of each hand pointing towards the person opposite. The cane is then laid across the outstretched fingers.

The cane must be lowered to the ground whilst remaining horizontal throughout. All team members must keep their fingers in contact with the cane at all times (no hooking of the cane is allowed).

Trust Exercises

Blind Walk

The students pair up and agree some form of non-verbal communication for directions, such as whistles, claps, finger clicks and so on. One of them is blindfolded and guided along a course by their partner, using only the pre-arranged signals.

Wind in the Willows

The team stands in a tight circle with one person in the middle. The person in the middle holds themselves as stiff and straight as they can, and falls in any direction, trusting spotters to catch him/her and stand him/her back up. The person in the middle should put their arms across their chest to avoid any inappropriate touching, and the task should be stopped immediately if it gets too boisterous.

Trust Fall

One student will be falling backwards from a wall, rock or other platform that is about waist height. The other students form two lines facing each other, with their arms out to catch the falling student. Ensure that the students have a good stance, there are no gaps in the catching arms, and they look down to avoid getting hit in the face. The falling student must hold their body stiff, and keep their arms by their sides to avoid hitting other students in the face.

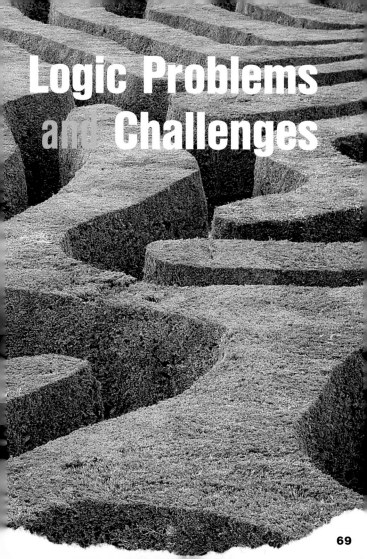

Logic Problems and Challenges

Logic Problems and Challenges

These require the students to think laterally and each can be run as an activity on its own, or to fill time.

Letter Dice

In the game of Letter Dice, a different letter of the alphabet is on each face of each of the 4 dice, so that 24 of the 26 letters of the alphabet occur. Words are formed by re-arranging and turning the dice, so that the top letters spell a 4-letter word. The 15 words below have been made using today's dice. Can you discover the 6 letters on each?

1. CAVE
2. CLEF
3. DUPE
4. FARE
5. FLUB
6. GREW
7. HAZY
8. KITH

9. LOIN
10. POEM
11. RASP
12. SMUG
13. TIRE
14. VARY
15. JAPE

Answers can be found on page 114

Missing Words

Every phrase in the following quiz has the words missing, but the first letter for each word has been given as a clue.

26 L of the A
= 26 Letters of the Alphabet

1.   29 **D** in **F** in a **L Y**
2.   7 **W** of the **W**
3.   1001 **A N**
4.   12 **S** of the **Z**
5.   54 **C** in a **P** (with the **J**)
6.   15 **M** on a **D M C**
7.   88 **P K**
8.   32 **D F** at which **W F**
9.   18 **H** on a **G C**
10. 90 **D** in a **R A**
11. 200 **P** for **P G** in **M**
12. 3 **B M** (**S H T R**)
13. 7 **S** on a **F P P**
14. 20 **N** on a **DB**
15. 1 **W** on a U
16. 57 **H V**
17. 11 **P** in a **F T**
18. 8850 **M**, **H** of **E**
19. 64 **S** on a **C B**
20. 147 **M B** in **S**
21. 8 **S** on an **O**
22. 876 **M** = **L E** to **J O'G**
23. 4 **S** in a **Y**
24. 10 **G B**, **S** on a **W**
25. 12 **N** on a **C F**

Answers can be found on page 115

NASA Survival Exercise

You are a member of a space crew originally scheduled to rendezvous with a mothership on the lighted surface of the moon. However, your ship was forced to land at a spot some 200 miles from the rendezvous point. Much of the equipment aboard was damaged and, since survival depends on reaching the mothership, the most critical items available must be chosen for the 200-mile trip. The 14 items left intact and undamaged after landing are listed opposite.

List the following 14 items in order of importance for your survival.

The answers can be found on page 116

- Box of matches
- Food concentrate
- 50 feet of nylon rope
- Parachute silk
- Portable heating unit
- Two .45 calibre pistols
- One case of dehydrated milk
- Two 100 lb tanks of oxygen
- Stellar map
- Magnetic compass
- 5 gallons of water
- Signal flares
- First aid kit, with injection needle
- Solar-powered two-way radio

Fox, Chicken and Grain

A farmer is standing on one bank of a river, with a fox, a chicken, and a bag of grain. He needs to get to the other side of the river, taking the fox, the chicken, and the grain with him. However, the boat used to cross the river is only large enough to carry the farmer and one of the things he needs to take with him, so he will need to make several trips in order to get everything across.

In addition, he cannot leave the fox unattended with the chicken, or else the fox will eat the chicken; and he cannot leave the chicken unattended with the grain, or else the chicken will eat the grain. The fox is not particularly partial to grain, and may be left alone with it. How can he get everything across the river without anything being eaten?

Students can act out the different roles to solve the problem.

Crossed or Uncrossed

The group sit in a circle and pass around two pens. As they do so, they must say whether they are crossed or uncrossed.

The leader tells each student if his or her statement was correct. It does not matter how the pens are passed, but if the person passing them has their legs (or other part of the body) crossed or not.

Man in the Moon

The idea behind this game is for the group to spot the link. At the start of the game, the leader says that the group will take it in turn to copy what they do, and they will tell them if they are right or not. Make sure that you do not say that they have to copy 'everything' as there is only one thing that they must copy to do the task correctly.

The leader says that there is an imaginary piece of chalk and that they will use it to draw a picture of the man in the moon. Tell one of the group that they have the piece of chalk, and ask them to pass it to you. Say "Thank You" when you receive it. Then proceed to draw with the imaginary chalk a large circle with two eyes and a mouth: the man in the moon.

The chalk is then passed around the circle, and members of the group attempt to copy the leader. If they have said "Thank You" when receiving the imaginary chalk, they have done it correctly, whatever else they may do after that. It may become necessary to exaggerate the "Thank You" on your demonstrations, if the group are getting frustrated.

Coins

This is a similar game to the previous one, in that the link is not obvious at first. Some coins are needed as props. Place some of the coins on a table and ask the group how many there are. Be careful not to say the word coins, as it is not the coins that they are counting, but the number of words in the question, like this:

"How many are there?"	= 4
"How many?"	= 2
"OK, how many are there in total now?"	= 8
(Just gesture toward the table)	= 0

Start off with the same number of words as coins, so that the group think it's obvious. Tell them if they are right or not, then change the number/arrangement of the coins. Keep going until most of the group have worked it out.

Wilderness
Survival Exercise

You and your companions have just survived the crash of a small plane. It is mid January, and you are in Northern Canada. The daily temperature is –32°C, and the night time temperature is –40°C. There is snow on the ground, and the countryside is wooded with several creeks crisscrossing the area. The nearest town is 20 miles away. You are all dressed in city clothes, appropriate for a business meeting.

Your group of survivors managed to salvage the following items:

- A ball of cotton wool
- A small axe
- A loaded .45-calibre pistol
- Metal can of Crisco shortening (vegetable fat)
- Newspapers (one per person)
- Cigarette lighter (without fluid)
- Extra shirt and trousers for each survivor
- 20×20ft piece of heavy-duty canvas
- A sectional air map made of plastic
- One quart of 100-proof whisky
- A compass
- Family-size chocolate bars (one per person)

List the 12 items above in order of importance for your survival.

The answers can be found on page 117

Guess Who

Each group member writes down the name of a famous person, and this name is attached to the forehead of another member of the group without them seeing the name. Attachment can be by sticky paper, such as a Post-It, using an elastic band, tucking it under the front of a hat, or even writing it on the forehead (with a washable pen!).

The members take it in turn to try and guess who they are. Answers to the questions can only be 'yes' or 'no' (though the leader can add a bit of information if necessary). If the answer is 'yes', then the person guessing gets another go. If it's a 'no' then the next person in the group guesses.

Story Time

The students are split into two groups and told that one group will invent a story, while the others wait outside the room. Once the other students return they can ask questions that have a 'yes' or 'no' answer to try and work out what the story is about.

No story is actually invented though. The students who remain in the room are told that the answers to the first two questions must be 'yes', and each third answer is a 'no'. This can result in some quite interesting stories!

Brainteasers/Riddles

1. Pronounced as one letter but written with three, only two different letters are used to make me. I'm double, I'm single, I'm black, blue, and grey. I'm read from both ends and the same either way.
   Answer: EYE.
2. What is the start of eternity and the end of time?
   Answer: The letter 'E'.
3. How can a woman legally marry 3 men, without ever getting a divorce, being widowed, or becoming legally separated?
   Answer: She's a priest.

4. Cathy has six pairs of black gloves and six pairs of brown gloves in her drawer. How many gloves must she take from the drawer in order to be sure to get a pair that match?
   Answer: 13.
   (She could possibly take out 6 black left hand gloves and then 6 brown left hand gloves, the next one would have to be a matching glove.)

5. Before Mt Everest was discovered, what was the highest mountain in the world?
   Answer: Mt Everest.

6. If there are 5 apples on the counter and you take away 2, how many do you have?
   Answer: 2 (the two that you took away!)

7. Jenn is facetious. She is also abstemious. She gets pneumonia. Given those clues, what is the only American tree she will like?
   Answer: The Sequoia. (She only likes words with all 5 vowels in them. The Sequoia is the only American tree that contains all 5 vowels.)

8. What English word can have 4 of its 5 letters removed and still retain its original pronunciation?
   Answer: Queue.

9. What goes up, and never comes down?
   Answer: Your age.

10. A woman goes into a hardware store to buy something for her house. When asked the price, the clerk replies, "The price of one is twelve pence, the price of forty-four is twenty-four pence, and the price of a hundred and forty-four is thirty-six pence. What does the woman want to buy?
    Answer: House numbers.

11. Johnny's mother had three children. The first child was named April. The second child was named May. What was the third child's name?
    Answer: Johnny, he's the third child.

12. If, having only one match, on a freezing winter's day, you entered a room that contained an oil lamp, a paraffin heater, and a wood burning stove, what would you light first.
    Answer: The match!

13. If three cats kill three rats in three minutes, how long will it take 100 cats to kill 100 rats?
    Answer: Three minutes.

14. A boat will carry only 200 pounds. How may a man weighing 200 pounds and his two sons, each weighing 100 pounds, use it to cross a river?
    Answer: Both sons row across, and one rows back. The father rows across. The son rows back and picks up his brother.

15. A monkey is at the bottom of a thirty foot well. Each day the monkey jumps up three feet and then slips down two. At that rate, how long will it take for the monkey to reach the top of the well?
    Answer: On day 28 he can jump to the top.

16. A rope ladder 10 feet long is hanging over the side of a ship. The rungs on the ladder are a foot apart, and the bottom rung is resting on the surface of the water. The tide rises at a rate of six inches an hour. When will the first three rungs be covered with water?
    Answer: They won't. The ladder rises with the ship.

17. The number of eggs in a basket doubles every minute. The basket is full of eggs after 10 minutes. When was the basket half full?
    Answer: After 9 minutes.

18. Which is correct; 8 and 8 **are** 15, or 8 and 8 **is** 15?
    Answer: Neither, 8 and 8 **equals** 16.

19. If all the walls on your house faced south, what colour would the bear outside be?
    Answer: White, because you live at the North Pole and it's a polar bear.

20. The person who makes it does not need it. The person who buys it does not use it. The person who uses it does so without knowing. What is it?
    Answer: A coffin, or a nappy.

Quiz

Teams write the answers down and swap for marking after each round. Some example questions are shown here. Picture and music rounds can also be planned.

TV

Q. What is the name of the Tweenies dog?

A. Doodles

Q. Which current children's show started in 1958?

A. Blue Peter

Q. How are Richard McCourt and Dominic Wood better known?

A. Dick and Dom

Q. What are the full names of the presenters of the show 'I'm a Celebrity. Get Me Out of Here?'

A. Anthony McPartlin and Declan Donnelly

Q. Who presents University Challenge?

A. Jeremy Paxman

Q. In which fictitious part of London is EastEnders set?

A. Walford

Q. Who plays Jack Bower in 24?

A. Kiefer Sutherland

Q. Which 3 cities are the CSI programmes set in?

A. Las Vegas, Miami and New York

Q. What programme does Peter Sissons appear on?

A. The News

Q. What's the name of the Simpsons' Family Doctor?

A. Dr Julius Hibbard

Movies

Q. What type of fish is Nemo in 'Finding Nemo'?

A. Clown Fish

Q. James Bond's double-0 licence allows him to do what?

A. Licence to Kill

Q. Who starred in 'The Matrix'?

A. Keanu Reeves

Q. Which actor's catchphrase is 'I'll be back'?

A. Arnold Schwarzenegger

Q. In the official series, how many actors have played James Bond?

A. Six

Q. Who are Bob Parr, Helen Parr, Dashiel Parr, Violet Parr and Jack Jack Parr known as?

A. The Incredibles

Q. Which character did Viggo Mortensen play in 'The Lord of the Rings?

A. Aragorn, or Strider

Q. Who played King Kong and Gollum?

A. Andy Serkis

Q. Which of these films did Alfred Hitchcock not direct; The Birds, The Haunting, Psycho, To Catch a Thief?

A. The Haunting

Q. Which two languages are used in 'The Passion of the Christ'?

A. Aramaic and Latin

Music

Q. Who is rapper Marshall Bruce Mathers the third?

A. Eminem

Q. Who had an album called '... Baby One More Time'?

A. Britney Spears

Q. Which primates from the north had a 'Favourite Worst Nightmare'?

A. Arctic Monkeys

Q. How many years were 'Take That' disbanded for?

A. 9

Q. Which of these is a Green Day song; Nasty Guys Finish Last, Pulling Hair, Basket Case, Welcome to Ponderosa?

A. Basket Case

Q. Which of the following is not a music format; WMA, AAC, MP3, TLA, WAV

A. TLA (Three Letter Acronym)

Q. How are dance music duo Edward Simons and Tom Rowlands better known?

A. Chemical Brothers

Q. What band was Bob Geldof in?

A. Boomtown Rats

Q. How old was Elvis when he died?

A. 42

Q. Which country was Mika born in?

A. Lebanon

Geography

Q. What is the capital city of Spain?

A. Madrid

Q. Which is further north, Toronto or Washington?

A. Toronto

Q. What colours are on the Irish Flag?

A. Green, White and Orange

Q. Switzerland is bordered by five countries; France, Germany and Italy are three of them, what are the other two?

A. Austria and Liechtenstein

Q. Which river is the longest; Yangtze, Nile or Amazon?

A. Nile

Q. Which American State is furthest south?

A. Hawaii

Q. In which country would you find Transylvania?

A. Romania

Q. What country is the world's second highest mountain, K2, in?

A. Pakistan

Q. In which Australian State or Territory is Ayers Rock/Uluru?

A. Northern Territory

Q. Which is the largest landlocked country in the world?

A. Kazakhstan

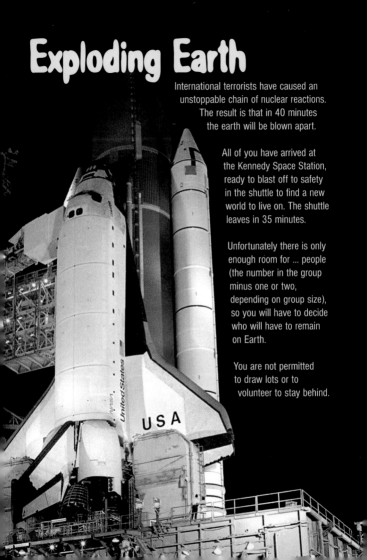

Exploding Earth

International terrorists have caused an unstoppable chain of nuclear reactions. The result is that in 40 minutes the earth will be blown apart.

All of you have arrived at the Kennedy Space Station, ready to blast off to safety in the shuttle to find a new world to live on. The shuttle leaves in 35 minutes.

Unfortunately there is only enough room for ... people (the number in the group minus one or two, depending on group size), so you will have to decide who will have to remain on Earth.

You are not permitted to draw lots or to volunteer to stay behind.

Each student is given a character and associated attributes. You will be given 5 minutes to put together a case, based on these factors, as to why you should be allowed to travel on the shuttle. You are not allowed to add characteristics. Each person is allowed to then put their case forward, and following that, the group will discuss and come to a unanimous decision before the time is up.

The two suggested criteria for the decision are:
1. The continuation of the human race
2. The individual's usefulness to the group

Personalities

Police Officer – carrying a gun, young, highly motivated and has a ten year old daughter

Vicar – kind and generous, intelligent with a degree in biochemistry

Army Officer – well organised, efficient and responsible, a natural leader

Pregnant Homemaker – trained health worker and spouse of the Police Officer

Insurance Clerk – young and well motivated, has been on a number of survival training courses

10-Year-Old Girl – daughter of Police Officer and Homemaker

45-Year-Old Female Politician – experienced in international affairs and negotiation techniques

Staff Nurse – fully trained in counselling, experience in delivering babies

Farmer – able to deal with crops and look after livestock

Retired Builder – aged 60, likes astronomy and designing models

Teacher – kind and bright, teaches modern languages, spouse of Staff Nurse

Doctor – a GP with over 20 years' experience and before those, 10 years at a General Hospital

Female Scientist – in her late 20s, PhD in chemistry, specialist subject is climatology

Student – studying physics at a top university, son of the Staff Nurse and Teacher

Construction Tasks

Some tasks that involve the team working together to construct something. A good activity for when it's raining.

Egg Drop

The students must construct something that will prevent a raw egg from breaking when dropped from a height, normally a first story window. The group are given some materials, such as paper, a plastic bag, straws, string, Sellotape, glue, paper clips, blue tack, and so on, depending on what you can get hold of. The designs will depend upon the construction materials available and the constraints put upon the team. The normal ideas are either a parachute, or a large round container with the egg suspended in the middle.

Some possible additional rules include:

- The construction must be completed before the egg is given to the group.
- A budget is given to the group, with each piece of material a set price. They must purchase their required materials.

Paper Aeroplane

The students must build a paper aeroplane.

The plane that flies the furthest wins.

Using a whole sheet of flipchart paper for each plane

can make the challenge more interesting.

Leaning Tower

Divide the students into equal-sized teams. They must build a tower that will support a plastic cup of water (or some other object) for 30 seconds. The highest tower that passes the test wins.

Materials could be straws, pins and blue tack, or paper, Sellotape and blue tack, or some other variation.

Paper Bridge

As for Leaning Tower, but this time building a bridge. The bridge must span a gap of 30cm between two tables, with the cup placed in the centre.

Fashion Show

The students are given two black rubbish bags, some tinfoil, and Sellotape with which to design and make an outfit for a fashion show.

One student is the model, and must walk down a 'catwalk' during the fashion show, with another student giving a commentary about the outfit. The outfit is judged and given a score.

Mini **Olympics**

This is basically a 'school sports day' type activity, with the only limitations on type of competition being safety and your own imagination. Depending on the group and the weather, these games can be quite wet and messy. Check with the landowner before trashing their field. Have someone keeping score and maybe have a scoreboard so the teams can see how they're doing.

There are the old classics of:

- Three legged race
- Sack race
- Egg and spoon race

Elements of Mini Olympics can require all the team, or representatives from the teams.

Egg Throwing

Those who want to compete pair up and are given a raw egg. The pairs line up so that they are in two straight lines facing their partner with a gap of 6ft. They then throw the egg across and catch it. Everyone takes a step back and the egg is thrown the other way, another step back, and so on. The winners are the pair who throw and catch their egg the furthest. Watch out for people throwing eggs at, rather than to, their partner. Have a bucket and cloth for cleaning up the mess.

Shoe Throw

Students throw one of their shoes (let them think it's just a distance competition). Once all are thrown, they are told to race and grab them, put on and do them up, and return to sit in their groups with their feet in the air.

Animal Relay

Each member of a team is allocated a different animal. They must then move during the race in the style of that animal. It's fun, but hard to score.

Donkey – Travelling on all fours to the goal and imitating the donkey's bray.

Duck – Walking on two feet in squat position, squawking without stopping. Arms out to sides as wings

Lame Dog – Walking on two hands and one foot and barking.

Bear – Bent over standing on their hands and feet, moves right hand and left foot together, and then left hand and right foot together.

Crab – Back toward the floor, supported on hands and feet. Must move sideways, like a crab.

Frog – Feet spread with his knees outside his hands, which are together. Advancing by frog-like jumps, landing on hands, then bringing the feet up.

Kangaroo Race

The first student grips a ball between their feet and hops around the course and back to their team. They hand over the ball and the next student goes.

Elephant Race

The first student runs to the end and back, then puts one hand between their legs for the second student to hold. They then run up and back together, and a third student joins the chain, and so on. If the chain breaks they must start again.

Back-to-Back Relay

Pairs standing back to back, their backs touching and arms linked, must run together to a goal and back with one running forward and the other running backward. If they separate, they must start over again.

Blindfold Race

This is a race for teams of three. Two are blindfolded, and clasp hands. The one not blindfolded holds their hands and guides them to the end and back.

Bucket Relay

Each team has two buckets. Fill one bucket half-full with water at the start, and leave the other empty at the far end. On 'Go', the first student carries the bucket to the end, pours the water into the other bucket, leaves the empty bucket there, and carries the water back to the next player in line. The winners are the first team to finish with their water intact.

Orange/Tennis Ball Race

The team stand in a line. The end person in the line holds the ball under their chin and passes it to the next in line (without the use of hands). The end person then runs to the front of the line. This continues until the whole team are past the finish line.

Wheels Relay

Each member of the team is given a number, and it's his or her turn to run when that number is called out. But they have to work out which number should run from the clue shouted out by the leader, before the leader shouts 'GO', for example:

1. Unicycle
2. Bicycle/Two Unicycles
3. Tricycle/Motor Bike and Unicycle/Steam Roller
4. Car/Two Bicycles/Trike and Unicycle
5. Tractor and Unicycle/Tricycle and Bicycle
6. Three Bicycles/Car including spare tyre and steering wheel

If the leader shouts "Train", everyone must run.

Nightline

A nightline course can be easily set up in an area of woodland, or anywhere else that there are enough objects to tie the string to. The students are simply blindfolded and have to follow the line around the course.

Care must be taken that the students are not going to injure themselves in any way, such as walking through holly or brambles, head-butting branches, falling down steep slopes.

An addition is to tie random objects onto the string along the course of the nightline, and at the end, challenge the group to identify the items in the correct order.

Hunts

Scavenger Hunt

Write a list of objects for the students to bring back and information for them to find out. These could be relevant to the group and the area. This can be run in two ways. Send off each team with the whole list and set a time for them to return. This is an easy way to run the activity, but allows students to mess about. Or split the list into small sections and give each team a part of the list. When they've completed their tasks they return, get marked on how well they've done and get given another list.

Sample Objects:
- Picture of the queen
- Six different leaves
- Six types of sweet (for the leaders to eat!)
- A feather
- A map of the world
- A ball
- A piece of leather

Sample Questions:
- How many bricks high is the building?
- What star sign would someone be if they were born today?
- How many miles is it to Edinburgh from here?
- What time did the sun rise today?

A–Z Hunt

The teams are each given an empty matchbox or film canister and told to find an object for every letter of the alphabet, with no object counting for two letters.

The problem is that all of these must fit in the container at the same time. It's easiest for the leader if the students have a written list of what they have put in the container.

Performance and Creative Activities

Performance and Creative Activities

Cheers/Yells

Have a Cheermaster (CM). Like a Ringmaster in a circus, they are someone who keeps control of the performance and encourages the students to cheer and applaud. Here are some ideas for cheers and clapping:

Yee Ha

The left side of the audience, (as looking from the stage) are told to shout **Yee** when the CM points to their side, the right to shout **Ha** when CM points to the right. So a quick point to left then right will result in a shout of **Yee Ha**. Variations can include length of shout as determined by how quickly the CM points, volume by the CM raising and lowering their hand and the obvious repetition of pointing to the right, **Ha Ha Ha**!

Competitions between sides on how loud they can get, and so on. Start with the basic shout and make it more complex as the performance goes on.

Clapping/Cheering

Use similar directions to Yee Ha – left and right sides of audience.

Tin Can

CM holds a can and the group cheer and applaud as the lid is removed from the can and become quiet as the lid is replaced.

Round of Applause
The group clap while moving their hands in a large circle.

Seal of Approval
The group hold their arms straight out in front of them, clap their hands and make "Arf Arf" noises like a seal.

Walking Chants
Chants can help a group to keep a good walking pace, and are fun to make up.

Sound Off

First part said by leader	second by team
Sound-off	1 – 2
Sound-off	3 – 4
1 – 2 – 3 – 4	1 – 2 (pause)
	3 – 4
One mile	no sweat.
Two miles	better yet.
Three miles	think about it.
Four miles	thought about it.
Five miles	feeling good like I should...

Sketch Show
A Sketch Show works best when the students are given time during the day to prepare their performances. The group should aim to make the sketch at least 10 minutes long but should not exceed 15 minutes. The sketch must be on a subject relating to the course, however tenuous the link. Students can be given a list of props they must make use of during the performance, for example, traffic cone, telephone directory, bin liner, pair of gloves.

You could also include a list of words or phrases to be incorporated, such as Catfish, Didgeridoo, The Arctic Circle, Homer Simpson.

The Sketch is a team event and a panel of Judges will assess the performance. Team marks will be awarded in the following categories: Artistic Impression, Content and Originality.

Marks will be deducted for: not using the props or phrases, short performance, excessive time wasting/padding, judge's discretion.

Comedy/Talent Show

The leaders should perform a few sketches at a talent show to get the group going. These are best practiced a few times to make them look good. Always check the quality of the 'talent' that the students have, help out with ideas, and warn them that it may be necessary to cut theirs short if the show is going over time – in other words, get them off the stage if they're really terrible!

Possible talents include: juggling, singing, playing a musical instrument, telling jokes (as long as they are not offensive), dancing, and so on.

You could also try variations on TV programmes, such as **Crimewatch**.

Crimewatch

You need to have a few people as different actors. An announcer says in a Crimewatch manner that a crime has been caught on camera and they're showing the tape to find out the culprits.

The victim walks on to the 'stage'. The two criminals rush on, beat up the victim, steal his wallet and run off.

The announcer says that they will replay it again at a slower speed to help with identification. The actors re-enact the robbery, slightly slower, but with slight differences, such as beating up the victim in a different way, wearing slightly different clothes, all stopping and smiling in a group photo way at the 'camera', and so on. Repeat a few times, slower, and with more extreme variations.

Cinderella

This needs a narrator, a Prince Charming and props.

Hear Ye! Hear Ye! Hear Ye! This is the word of Prince Charming (1), ruler (2) over this land (3). Let it be known that Prince Charming (1) does seek a beautiful maiden (4) who has lost her slipper (5). No, I said slipper, not flipper (6).

Last night the Prince (1) did hold a ball (7), it was a joyous occasion (8), but lo! (9). At the stroke of one (10). The maiden did run away, and the Prince (1) did declare the ball was off (11).

So the Prince (1) shall not rest. He shall search high and low (12), near and far, and up and down this land (13), and let it be known that he shall comb the hillocks (14), and he shall comb the valleys (15) until he shall find the beautiful maiden whom the flipper will fit (16). This the Prince knows (17), and he shall pick the right one (18). When he has picked the right one (19) the Prince wishes to marry her.

So, be prepared ye people, for the Prince (1) shall come among you, and he shall try it on with every young maiden in the land (20). He shall try the flipper upon tall maidens, upon small maidens, and upon maidens stupid enough to sit near the front, until he finds the maiden whom the flipper will fit (21), and he shall lead the maiden onto the stage (22).

The Prince shall ask the maiden her name (23). The Prince shall love her deeply (24). She shall be so deep in gratitude that she shall kiss him deeply upon his luscious lips (25). The Prince shall mount the maiden (26) upon his horse (27) and they shall live happily ever after.

The End (28)

Actions and Props

1. Slap thigh, point to self with thumbs and smile cheekily
2. Pull out a ruler from sock
3. Make a sweeping, over the hills motion with hand
4. Make hour glass figure shape with hands
5. Pull out a snorkelling flipper from back of trousers (or a kitchen flipper utensil)
6. Shrug shoulders
7. Put hand in a trouser pocket containing a small ball
8. Smile at the audience
9. Push hand further down into pocket
10. Stroke the pocket the ball is in
11. Look worried, then pull ball out of pocket, and drop it
12. Look high, and down low
13. Look around stage
14. Take out a comb and comb chest hair
15. Pretend to comb backside
16. Make hour glass figure shape with hands
17. Point to nose
18. Put finger up right nostril
19. Pull out finger
20. Start to try flipper on maidens as narrator continues
21. Find someone to take on stage (Leader?)
22. Lead Cinderella onto the stage
23. Ask her name
24. Smile at the audience
25. Shut eyes and pucker up!
26. Smile at the audience
27. Offer Cinderella a piggy-back lift
28. Bow to the audience

Makeshift glass slippers

Songs

Singing can help motivate a team during an activity, and pass the time while sitting around a campfire. Songs can be classic campfire songs, nursery rhymes, chart songs or any other song that most of the group know, or that someone can lead. By dividing the group into sections a song can be sung as a round, in other words, section two starts the first line as section one are starting the second, the classic song for this being campfire's burning.

Campfire's Burning
(to the tune of London's Burning)

Campfire's burning, campfire's burning
Draw nearer, draw nearer
In the gloaming, in the gloaming
Come sing and be merry

Alice the Camel
Alice the camel has five humps
Alice the camel has five humps
Alice the camel has five humps
So go Alice go!

...repeat counting down until...

Alice the camel has no humps
Alice the camel has no humps
Alice the camel has no humps
Because Alice is a horse!

Father Abraham

Father Abraham had seven sons
Seven sons had Father Abraham
And they wouldn't laugh
And they wouldn't cry

All they did was go like this...
with a left (arm moving)...

(repeat song, keep adding actions)... With a left (arm) and a right (arm).

Finally:... with a left and a right, and a left (leg) and a right (leg), and a nod, and a wiggle.

'Repeat After Me' Songs
(leader sings the line, everyone repeats)

Boom Chicka Boom

I said a boom!
I said a boom chicka boom!
I said a booma chicka rocka chicka rocka chicka boom!
Uh huh!
Oh yeah!

One more time...
(state the type, examples below)

* Underwater: with fingers dribbling against your lips
* Loud: as loud as you can!
* Quiet: whispering
* Slowly: as slow and drawn out as possible
* Quickly: really fast
* American Accent, Australian, and so on

Verses with Special Words:

Janitor Style:
I said a broom.
I said a broom pusha broom.
I said a broom pusha mopa pusha mopa pusha broom...

Barnyard Style:
I said a moo.
I said a moo chicka moo.
I said a moo chicka oink chicka oink chicka moo...

Flower Style:
I said a bloom.
I said a bloom chicka bloom.
I said a bloom chicka blossom chicka blossom chicka bloom...

Racing Car Style:
I said a vroom.
I said a vroom shifta vroom.
I said a vroom shifta grinda shifta grinda shifta vroom...

Astronaut Style:
I said a moon.
I said a shoot me to the moon.
I said a shoot me blast me shoot me blast me shoot me to the moon...

Yellow Bird

I saw a bird with a yellow bill
Was perched upon my window sill
I coaxed him in with a piece of bread
And then I stroked his little head

Add extra verses, for example
'...can of Tizer',
'Put him in a liquidiser'.

Story Telling

Someone starts a story and, after a couple of sentences, the leader 'spins the bottle' to decide on someone else to continue the story. It's more fun if you go fast. The wilder the story, the better.

Another approach is to go around the circle with each person adding the next two words to the story. You can increase the number of words each person says to make it easier and flow better.

Presentations

Leaders can give a presentation on some aspect of the activities that the group are taking part in. This can be good practice for those leaders who need to give presentations as part of their assessment for qualifications, and can be used to cover parts of the curriculum if teachers require it.

Possible topics could include:

- Lead climbing, with an explanation of a lead rack, and clips from a video, such as the start of **Hard Grit**!
- An introduction to kayaking on moving water with a description of types of river features.
- Winter mountaineering and avalanches. How to find people and avoid being avalanched.

In order to maintain interest, in case the speaker isn't very good, a quick quiz on the subject could be planned for after the talk, with the winning team/pair/individual getting some sort of reward.

Useful Books and Websites

I like reading books and playing on the Internet, so here's a list of some books and websites I'd recommend:

Canoeing and Kayaking

- BCU **Canoe and Kayak Handbook and Coaching Handbook**
- **Kayak and Canoe Games** by David Ruse and Loel Collins
- www.ukriversguidebook.co.uk
- www.canoewales.com

Caving

- **Complete Caving Handbook** by Andy Sparrow
- www.ukcaves.co.uk

Climbing

- **Rockclimbing** – MLTUK Volume 2
- **The Complete Guide to Rope Techniques** by Nigel Shepherd
- www.ukclimbing.com
- www.thebmc.co.uk

Expedition Training

- **How to Shit in the Woods** by Kathleen Meyer
- www.jfk.herts.sch.uk/extra_curric/dofe/expedition_training/index.htm

First Aid

- **Surviving a Career in Adventure Activities** – AAIAC
- www.hse.gov.uk/pubns/indg347.pdf

Games

- **Quicksilver** by Karl Rohnke and Steve Butler (and all other Karl Rohnke books)
- www.youthwork-practice.com

Guidebooks

- www.v-outdoor.co.uk
- www.v-publishing.co.uk

Mountaineering

- **Hillwalking** – MLTUK Volume 1
- **Winter Skills** – MLTUK Volume 3
- **Mountain Navigation** by Peter Cliff

Presentations

- www.presentationzen.com

Reviewing

- www.reviewing.co.uk
- www.mysite.wanadoo-members.co.uk/outdoor

Skiing

- **Pock'it Instructor** by Sally Chapman

Songs

- www.scoutingresources.org.uk/song_index.html

Weather

- **Mountain Weather** – www.mwis.org.uk

Wide Games

- www.edinburgh-scout.org.uk/games/gc9.html

Answers

Page 70

Letter Dice Problem – Answers:

The faces on the four dice are

- A-D-L-M-T-W
- B-E-K-N-S-Y
- C-H-J-O-R-U
- F-G-I-P-V-Z

Missing Word Problem – Answers:

1. 29 Days in February in a Leap Year
2. 7 Wonders of the World
3. 1001 Arabian Nights
4. 12 Signs of the Zodiac
5. 54 Cards in a Pack with the Jokers
6. 15 Men on a Dead Man's Chest
7. 88 Piano Keys
8. 32 Degrees Fahrenheit at which Water Freezes
9. 18 Holes on a Golf Course
10. 90 Degrees in a Right Angle
11. 200 Pounds for Passing Go in Monopoly
12. 3 Blind Mice
    (See How They Run)
13. 7 Sides on a Fifty Pence Piece
14. 20 Numbers on a Dart Board
15. 1 Wheel on a Unicycle
16. 57 Heinz Varieties
17. 11 Players in a Football Team
18. 8850 Metres, Height of Everest
19. 64 Squares on a Chess Board
20. 147 Maximum Break in Snooker
21. 8 Sides on an Octagon
22. 876 Miles = Land's End to John O'Groats
23. 4 Seasons in a Year
24. 10 Green Bottles,
    Sitting on a Wall
25. 12 Numbers on a Clock Face

NASA Survival Exercise – Answers

1. Oxygen – Most pressing survival need
2. Water – Needed for liquid loss on the light side
3. Map – Primary means of navigation
4. Food – Energy requirements
5. Two-way radio – For communication with mother ship
6. Rope – For climbing and making slings or stretchers
7. First Aid Kit – Needles fit NASA space suit
8. Silk – Protection from the sun's rays
9. Flares – Use as distress signal
10. Pistols – Possible means of self-propulsion
11. Milk – Bulky food concentrate
12. Heating – Only needed on the dark side
13. Compass – Moon's magnetic field is not polarised
14. Matches – Useless, no oxygen on the moon

Scoring: For each item, mark the number of points that your score differs from the NASA ranking, then add up all the points. Disregard plus or minus differences. The lower the total, the better your score.

0 – 25 excellent
26 – 32 good
33 – 45 average
46 – 55 fair
56 – 70 poor
71 – 112 very poor

Page 77

Wilderness Survival Exercise – Answers

1. Cigarette lighter – Create sparks for fire
2. Ball of cotton wool – Catching sparks, or for wound dressing
3. Extra clothes – Warmth, and for shelter, signalling, bedding, bandages, and fuel for the fire
4. Vegetable fat – Many uses for the can, and oil can be used as fuel
5. Canvas – Used as a shelter
6. Small axe – To get fuel for fire, and build a shelter
7. Chocolate – Food energy.
8. Newspapers – Starting a fire, and insulation under clothing. Used as reading material for recreation.
9. Pistol – A signalling device, sound of shots fired. The butt of the pistol could be used as a hammer.
10. Whisky – Fire building and as a fuel for a torch.
11. Compass – Due to temperature best to wait for rescue. Signalling device, reflecting sunlight.
12. Air map – Least desirable, it will encourage individuals to try to walk to help. Can be used to keep someone dry.

Scoring: For each item, mark the number of points that your score differs from the answers, and then add up all the points. Disregard plus or minus differences. The lower the total, the better your score.

Your notes and additions

ENJOY THE OUTDOORS

Come and see our full range of outdoor books, maps and guides.

www.**v-outdoor**.co.uk

VERTEBRATE **OUTDOOR**